Sharan Bhachu is a family law practitioner, whose practice has a particular emphasis on child protection work. She is regularly instructed on behalf of parents, local authorities and children's guardians and has developed a reputation for being straightforward and forthright. Sharan's experience in public law is extensive, ranging from emergency protection orders to secure accommodation orders and discharging care orders. Similarly, her experience in private law is also wide-ranging and includes declarations of parentage and all aspects of abduction, Hague and non-Hague Convention related and Forced Marriage.

Sharan has considerable experience in allegations of sexual abuse, physical domestic violence and non-accidental injury cases, including where the injuries were caused by rare genetic mutations, and has often represented interveners in such cases. She has experience in cross-examining a wide range of experts, including medical experts, and is also experienced in cases involving transgender and cultural issues and factitious illness. She has particular experience in complex matters involving the forensic analysis of often disputed expert evidence.

A Practical Guide to Factitious Illness in Care Proceedings

A Practical Guide to Factitious Illness in Care Proceedings

Sharanjeet Kaur Bhachu

Barrister

LLB (Hons)

Law Brief Publishing

Published 2023 by Law Brief Publishing, an imprint of Law Brief Publishing Ltd
30 The Parks
Minehead
Somerset
TA24 8BT

www.lawbriefpublishing.com

Paperback: 978-1-914608-42-1

To Biji and Babaji and all those before us who sacrificed so much to enable us to have opportunities.

PREFACE

Much of an advocates job is learned whilst on our feet. Having a reference guide to go to for some of the more complex areas is a must for all advocates of all different levels of experience.

The law quoted in this book is accurate as at the 1st March 2023.

Sharan Bhachu
March 2023

CONTENTS

Chapter One	Defining Factitious Illness Disorders	1
	Introduction	1
	Medically unexplained symptoms (MUS)	5
	Perplexing presentations	5
	Other factitious disorders	6
	- Malingering	6
	- Somatic symptom disorders (SSD)	7
	Summary	8
Chapter Two	How Do FII Cases Fit Within Care Proceedings: Pre-Proceedings	9
	Perplexing Presentations (PP) / Fabricated or Induced Illness (FII) in Children RCPCH Guidance	10
	- Alerting signs	11
	- Health and Education Rehabilitation Plans	13
	- Responsible Consultant and Named and Designated professionals	15
	- Record keeping and Chronologies	17
	Safeguarding Children in whom illness is fabricated or induced' - The 2008 Guidance	17
	Summary	23

Chapter Three	Threshold and Fact-Finding	25
	Recognition of which type of FII is involved	25
	Preparation of the papers	28
	Pleading of thresholds and schedule of findings	30
	Further legal considerations	38
	Covert Recordings	45
	- Recordings by parents/carers	45
	- Covert Video Surveillance	47
	- Intimate Images	48
	Summary	51
Chapter Four	Post-Fact Finding	55
	Harm to children	56
	What now?	58
	Summary	63
	Conclusion	63

CHAPTER ONE

DEFINING FACTITIOUS ILLNESS DISORDERS

Introduction

Munchausen's and Munchausen's by proxy, factitious illness (FII), medically unexplained symptoms and perplexing presentations are all terms which are banded around without any real clear meaning to what they exactly relate to and often strike fear into the hearts of practitioners before they have even begun to understand what may be happening within an unusual or unexplained family situation. Understanding the proper definition of this group of disorders is key to identifying and understanding what may be going on. These cases have very unusual features and require a different depth of knowledge and understanding alongside that of any other type of care proceedings. The aim of this book is to provide a level of resource to allow practitioners who are instructed on such cases to understand the context of such cases and the best ways in which to present the best possible case for whichever party they are instructed to represent.

The Royal College of Paediatrics and Child Health (RCPCH) have, as of March 2021, updated their guidance on FII[1]. They had introduced the term of perplexing presentations in 2013 and expand on this with additional material to support management in the latest

---

1 RCPCH 'Fabricated or induced illness by carers: A practical guide for paediatricians' February 2021 https://childprotection.rcpch.ac.uk/resources/perplexing-presentations-and-fii/

version. The guidance is an invaluable source of information for all practitioners involved in cases whereby FII of some sort or another is suspected, ranging from social workers/professionals and those representing family members or a child.

As referenced above, factitious or induced illness or disorder is, in fact, a group of disorders. Historically factitious disorders were conjointly referred to as Munchausen's[2] or Munchausen's by proxy[3]. This did not help the identification or understanding of often complex and often subtly nuanced situations and many professionals went on to adopt the terms of factitious illness/disorders, which is now used universally. The RCPCH have used the term 'Fabricated or induced illness' since the early 2000's and professionals and practitioners have been actively discouraged from using the terms Munchausen's as a catch-all.

The most recent DSM-5[4] defines factitious disorder in the following two ways:

Factitious disorder imposed on self

A. Falsification of physical or psychological signs or symptoms, or induction of injury or disease, associated with identified deception.

---

2 Originally named by Asher R, : Munchausen's syndrome', The Lancet, 1951, 1: 339-341

3 Then named by Meadow R, [1977] 'Munchausen Syndrome by Proxy: The hinterland of child abuse". The Lancet, 310 98033, pp 343-345

4 The Diagnostic and Statistical Manual of Mental Disorders, Fifth Edition [2013] American Psychiatric Association

B. *The individual presents himself or herself to others as ill, impaired, or injured.*

C. *The deceptive behavior is evident even in the absences of obvious external rewards.*

D. *The behaviour is not better explained by another mental disorder, such as delusional disorder or another psychotic disorder.*

Factitious disorder imposed on another (previously Disorder by proxy):

A. *Falsification of physical or psychological signs or symptoms, or induction of injury or disease, in another, associated with identified deceptions.*

B. *The individual presents another individual (victim) to others as ill, impaired, or injured.*

C. *The deceptive behaviour is evident even in the absences of obvious external rewards.*

D. *The behaviour is not better explained by another mental disorder, such as delusional disorder or another psychotic disorder.*

In cases involving FII on self, the attention is focused on the adult who presents themselves with deliberate, feigned or exaggerated symptoms. FII on another, will present with the focus on another – a child/ren for our purposes. FII on another is also referred to as either fabricated (whereby the carer deliberately makes up and reports false symptoms of an illness) FII or induced (whereby the carer deliberately induces symptoms of an illness). Whichever disorder is present, it is the motive that is relevant to the welfare issues for the child. The motive of a perpetrator of FII, whether on themselves or another is to present themselves or another with factitious symptoms, behaviours or illnesses in order to gain the role of an ill person or a carer of an ill child. The more complex issue of the reasoning behind that motive is considered later in this book.

The RCPCH guidelines make a clear distinction between FII being a clinical situation where there may or may not be intent, if intent is not clear, and those situations whereby evidence is available to indicate that the motivation on behalf of the carer is to convince the medical professionals that the child has the illness, with recurring presentations to health and other professionals. The latter clearly forms abuse and child protection procedures are triggered.

It is also of note that although induction is and can be considered a form of physical abuse, the relevant factor is the motive of the carer and is almost always accompanied with repeated and recurrent presentations to professionals which then allows it to be considered under the umbrella of FII.

It is noteworthy that the diagnosis on the latter relates not to the person/child being presented as ill but the person presenting them. This is another example of the clear intention by professionals involved in child protection to move the focus away from the child and onto the perpetrator, allowing the overriding objective of care proceedings and child protection in general – that of the best interests and welfare of the child – to be met.

So when a carer deliberately causes a child to display symptoms of a particular illness or general unwellness to gain medical attention, it is important to note how that deception or inducement is happening. Often there are three main forms; fabrication, falsification or inducement. This could be of medical records, results or symptoms and can lead to unneeded procedures and treatments being provided to the child as the doctors to whom the child has been presented make efforts to understand and treat them. In very serious cases, the child may have been poisoned or the perpetrator may have tampered with medical equipment or medication prescribed to the child in good faith and based on the false history given by the carer.

Medically unexplained symptoms (MUS)

The range of possible scenarios within the factitious disorder spectrum is wide and far reaching. Not every situation will present as a result of an intentional deception yet identified deception is a clear and necessary part of the DSM diagnosis. It is too simple a definition and doesn't cover many of the situations that arise in these complex care cases. Practitioners and social care/medical professionals may be faced with situations whereby the child presents with symptoms that are not as a result of deception but are in fact genuinely felt or experienced. Such symptoms may be of a psychosocial nature or a 'functional disorder'. Often the carers are not involved in any form of induction of these symptoms or even any kind of deception and are fully able to work with the professionals involved to help and treat the underlying causes. These situations have evolved to become known and referred to as 'medically unexplained symptoms' (MUS), However, MUS does not automatically mean that FII is excluded.

Perplexing presentations

The RCPCH introduced the term 'perplexing presentations' (PP) to identify situations whereby FII (actual harming of children likely to amount to significant harm) has not yet occurred but there are concerning signs of discrepancies between the state of the child as reported by the carers and the independent observations and presentations of the child to medical professionals. These are the cases that often present as the most difficult to identify, with many children having a degree of underlying illness and therefore proving exaggeration in symptoms by the carer can prove to be very difficult. There is often significant involvement of many medical and other professionals, medical records and reported observations and presentations that may or may not have been independently observed. Perplexing presentation may well manifest well before any significant harm under the umbrella of FII is caused to the child but is likely in itself to cause repeated harm to the child.

These are issues which often arise in the context of private law disputes, whereby the threshold is not yet crossed to warrant the involvement of social services but is enough to instigate the appointment of a Rule 16.4 guardian to represent the child. Advocates should always be alive to the need for separate representation when there is a suspicion of perplexing presentations. Anything more serious that ventures into suspected FII territory may require consideration of a Section 37 report. The need for expert assessment should also be kept under consideration.

Other factitious disorders

Practitioners will also come other disorders that fall under the umbrella of being factitious but may or may not be recognized disorders. These often have a much less sinister connotation and usually solve unexplained situations with ease once identified. It is of note that these types of disorders are likely to manifest themselves on a much more obvious basis and should always be kept in mind.

Malingering

This is a disorder whereby the adult pretends to have an illness with the clear intention to procure a material benefit for themselves or to avoid a responsibility such as caring for a child.

Both malingering and FII require intentional deception but the difference between factitious disorder and malingering appear ***in the reason*** for the deception, which in malingering is tangible and rationally understandable. This is a complete contrast to FII whereby the motivation is to either take the role of being ill or as a carer of an ill child.

Malingering is not considered a mental illness and does not have any diagnostic criteria, therefore it does not require an expert to diagnose, and practitioners may consider whether findings of fact by a Judge are required to determine the truth of matter. An extreme example of this can be seen in cases whereby a parent who makes allegations that their child is being or has been sexually and/or physically abused by the separated parent in order to obviously avoid a relationship or contact with the other parent and child. These children are often presented at hospital or to the GP with repeated unverified reports of signs of sexual abuse and it can be very difficult to ascertain whether there is a psychological component or whether this is a straightforward type of malingering/parental alienation. The key is always in the detail.

Somatic symptom disorders (SSD)

These disorders tend to relate to presentations of illness or symptoms of the body rather than the mind but are often in fact an interplay between the psychological and the physical. The person may genuinely feel the pain or symptoms associated with a particular illness which clearly does not exist. It is unlikely to be intentional and the psychological component is highly relevant.

Summary

Having an idea of the range of conditions and disorders that come under the factitious umbrella is imperative for practitioners involved in these cases. These are cases that often do not make any sense to anyone around the family or there may be suspicions but no hard evidence to back up any referrals or pleading of the case, if at the stage of proceedings. Many social workers have not come across cases involving FII and while instinct is telling them that something is not right, they are often not experienced enough to identify that FII may well be the issue. Careful analysis and consideration of the records, not just medication or treatment related but the observations and presentations is vital to understanding how best to identify the issues and then consider how best to move forwards to safeguard and protect. The well-known cases such as salt poisoning are obvious and much more readily identifiable but it is the more nuanced, entrenched families whereby suspicions are raised but never amount to much more either because the carer changes tack or moves to a different area, often resulting in a confused and complicated set of records that require a forensic detailed analysis.

CHAPTER TWO

HOW DO FII CASES FIT WITHIN CARE PROCEEDINGS: PRE-PROCEEDINGS

If a child is deemed to be suffering or at risk of harm, the normal course of events is for a referral to social services to be made. In FII cases the referral will often be made by a GP, health visitor or hospital when over a period of time those same professionals have suspicions that a child is being presented for medical attention but the observations of the child do not match with the symptoms that the carer states the child has or where the child is not responding to treatment or medication in the way expected.

As practitioners who have been instructed on a case that may involve FII, it is as important to understand what should have happened pre-proceedings as it is to understand how to move forward. This chapter covers what should have been happening before the case even reaches the stage of being issued.

The majority of these types of cases, if not all, will come under the radar of professionals who are engaged in child protection alongside their usual employment; teachers, medical professionals, GPs, health visitors to name a few. There are many protocols and guidance in relation to safeguarding children in general and more specifically in relation to FII. The two most important are considered in further detail below and although the salient points have been taken out for the purposes of this book, an advocate who has read many times the two documents is in a more advantageous position than any other professional in the room, regardless of who is being represented.

It is also the prepared advocate who will make sure they are relying on the most up to date version of the guidance as well as understanding the interplay between them both.

Perplexing Presentations (PP)/Fabricated or Induced Illness (FII) in Children RCPCH Guidance

On the 2nd March 2021, the Royal College of Paediatrics and Child Health published the most recent version of their FII specific guidance which was last published in 2009[5]. The guidance was revised for a number of reasons , not least that the Department of Education was not planning to revise its multi-agency guidance and there was increasing concern amongst professionals as to the need for the inclusion of perplexing presentations as an evolving concept and how to deal with those situations. The specific aim of the guidance was to have clear definitions of the various conditions/disorders and provide clear practical advice, mainly to paediatricians, but highly relevant to all child protection professionals, as to how to recognise and respond in order to safeguard and improve outcomes for children. Importantly there was a clear recognition that the concerning behaviour of the carer may not always be deception but triggered by anxiety or a false belief about the child's state of health, with access to internet searches becoming more and more common and almost always being extremely unhelpful.

The guidance helpfully sets out the essential principles at chapter 1.2 and is essential reading. Some of the most relevant parts for legal practitioners are considered in more detail below.

5 https://childprotection.rcpch.ac.uk/resources/perplexing-presentations-and-fii/

Alerting signs

The Guidance deals at length with alerting signs at chapter 4.4. In themselves they are not considered evidence of clear FII but may be indicators and therefore professionals should be alert and ready to further investigate. One alone is unlikely to amount to any real concern and the emphasis is on looking at the bigger picture to see if there is any evidence of a picture of alerting signs, with further analysis of their severity and frequency.

Alerting signs may be found in either the child's presentation, whether it be physical, psychological or in their behaviour.

- Initial contact with professionals made on the basis of symptoms that are not observed by the health professionals they have been brought to see;
- Unexpected/poor responses to recommended treatment that cannot be explained by the professionals given the reported symptoms;
- Parts of the reported illness/symptoms that simply cannot be explained medically;;
- Difficulties with social interaction and reducing or lack of school attendance.

They can also be present in the carers behaviour:

- insistence on continued investigations despite medical recommendations being given for treatment and being ineffective or where the reported symptoms and signs are not explained by any known medical condition in the child;
- not allowing the child to speak to their conditions/symptoms;

- Repeated reporting of new symptoms;
- Not wanting the child to be seen;
- Recurring presentations at medical settings, whether the GP, Health Visitor, hospitals, treating physicians;
- seeking multiple medical opinions;
- Actively seeking and presenting reports by other health professionals , often in in conflict with UK medical practice or the specific issues being raised;
- Non-attendance at some or all appointments;
- Inability in accepting reassurance or agreement to recommended management, often accompanied with insistence of pursuit of non-recommended treatments, investigations that may have no or questionable medical basis;
- Objections to communication between professionals;
- Frequent complaints about professionals.

Although not exhaustive, the above give a good range of indicators of the types of behaviours that are considered as the most common[6] of alerting signs and the perusal of papers by an advocate will be able to establish the presence of any of these from the medical notes, observations of professionals and communications between the carers and the professionals. Professionals may not have picked up on all of

6 See also the NICE guidelines for Fabricated or induced Illness, Child Maltreatment – recognition and management January 2019

the alerting signs and given them further investigation by the time the lawyers are involved and so it is important not to miss what may be the beginning of a much bigger picture that hasn't been clear so far.

Interestingly, at this part of the Guidance there is specific reference to consideration of any adverse experiences either by the child or carer/s and the need to consider the impact of these on the behaviours as described above. In fact the Guidance goes as far as to state that the medical professionals should 'explicitly explore whether the child is currently experiencing, or has previously experienced, adverse childhood experiences such as physical, sexual or emotional abuse, neglect, domestic abuse, child sexual or criminal exploitation, bereavement, parental/caregiver alcohol or drug misuse, severe parental mental health issues or a parent going to prison[7]" with additional guidance that this may also apply to the carer.

Health and Education Rehabilitation Plans

Professionals working together need to be aiming to identify the medical/psychosocial picture for the child with discussion and cooperation across the board of professionals involved with the child and family. Multi professional meetings are considered necessary so that consensus can be reached, avoiding any binary thinking about the physical and psychosocial aspects that may have been identified. The Guidance rightly recognises that the physical and psychosocial are often interlinked and so any plan going forward must consider them both with input from all those who know and are involved with the child. The Guidance sets out the process to be followed and is helpful

7 4.5 of the RCPCH guidance

for advocates in considering cross examination or exploration of witnesses as to how certain conclusions or decisions came to be reached;

> *"In order to resolve these concerns, a decision needs to be made about whether the perplexing presentation is explained and resolved by a verified medical condition in the child, or whether concerns remain.*
>
> *In order to resolve this, a consensus needs to be reached in a meeting between all professionals about the following issues:*
>
> *Either*
>
> - *That all the alerting signs and problems are explained by verified physical and/or psychiatric pathology or neurodevelopmental disorders in the child and there is no FII (false positives).*
> - *Medically Unexplained Symptoms from the child free from parental suggestion*
> - *That there are perplexing elements but the child will not come to harm as a result.*
>
> *Or*
>
> *And agree all of the following*
>
> - *Whether further investigations and seeking of further medical opinions is warranted in the child's interests*
> - *How the child and the family need to be supported to function better alongside any remaining symptoms, using a Health and Education Rehabilitation Plan*

- *If the child does not have a secondary care paediatric Consultant involved in their care, consideration needs to be given to involving local services*

- *The health needs of siblings*

- *Next steps in the eventuality that parents disengage or request a change of paediatrician in response to the communication meeting with the responsible paediatric consultant about the consensus reached and the proposed Health and Education Rehabilitation Plan."*[8]

Such meetings are required to be properly minuted and it should be possible from perusal of the medical disclosure to understand the thought process of each of the professionals involved and the evolution of conclusions and management being reached. The reality is that the same perusal often provides much fodder for cross examination of witnesses who were either unaware of their duties, were aware but failed to follow them through or had clear views that were followed rather than the process.

Responsible Consultant and Named and Designated professionals

The Guidance makes clear the need for a named doctor to take the role of a 'Responsible Consultant', one that is usually the doctor with the main care for the child and who will be responsible for liaising with all other medical health professionals and collating information as to the current health involvement.

The reality is that for many of these situations there is a Consultant Paediatrician or Child psychiatrist involved already but the Guidance

8 5.3.1 of the RCPCH guidance

also makes clear that in the unusual circumstance that there isn't, the professionals should make a referral to one to become the named responsible Consultant.

There is even clear stipulation that in complex cases there should be consideration of someone other than the main treating Doctor to ensure objectivity going forward and there is further recognition that sometimes an unhealthy and very unhelpful collusive or unprofessional relationship can be formed between the carers and health professional. Another factor often arises when the carer resorts to multiple and frequent complaints about the health professional, causing significant difficulties in the relationship.

Why is this an important and relevant factor for lawyers? The RCPCH guidance has always considered the need for not only named Responsible Consultants but also Named and Designated Professionals, who "are responsible for supporting the responsible consultant and the clinical team, for oversight of the safeguarding aspects of the child's care and for achieving a health consensus" for the child. These are important individuals who are able to collate and communicate with the often numerous health professionals who are involved, who are able to collate the bigger picture and see whether the threshold for concerns re FII and referral to social care is required.

Failure to appoint a Responsible Consultant often leads to mismanagement of the child's care, a lack of linking up of the reporting of concerns and symptoms by the carer and sometimes misguided concerns as to there being FII simply because the bigger picture is being not being seen. Once the stigma of a suspicion or allegation of FII appears, it usually snowballs and becomes a label that is hard to remove.

Unpicking the mess that often is presented due to a lack of training or overzealous health and social care professionals is especially complex and difficult without any foundational knowledge of this area.

Record keeping and Chronologies

The Guidance confirms that record keeping is essential, that it should record who reported concerns and what was actually observed and by whom. The need for clear and recorded communication between all professionals and with parents is vital going forward and that records must show what was and what wasn't discussed with parents.

Chronologies are also recommended, although accepted that they are not necessary for every case and these will be discussed in further detail in chapter 3.

***Safeguarding Children in whom illness is fabricated or induced' –* The 2008 Guidance**

The RCPCH guidance is specifically aimed at Paediatricians and needs to be considered alongside other more mainstream Guidance for professionals involved in child protection and safeguarding.

The Department for children, schools and families published in 2008 guidance called *'Safeguarding Children in whom illness is fabricated or induced'*[9] [The 2008 Guidance]. This recognises the importance of professionals working together given these situations are rare and often misunderstood. The purpose of the guidance was to build upon guidance and assessment frameworks already set out in the *Working*

9 https://www.londonsafeguardingchildrenprocedures.co.uk/files/sg_ch_fab_ill.pdf

Together to Safeguard Children: A guide to inter-agency working to safeguard and promote the welfare of children[10] and the *Framework for the Assessment of Children in need and their families*[11] and aimed to provide a standard of good practice that should have been incorporated by all Local Safeguarding Children's Boards[12] to ensure better outcomes for children and versions of the guidance can be found on the websites of all local authorities.

The guidance sets out four areas in which effective measures in safeguarding need to be considered alongside the wider availability of support and services available;

- *Many of the families in which a child has had illness fabricated or induced have experienced a number of stress factors in their lives. Providing services and support to these families may strengthen the capacity of parents to respond to the needs of these children before they reach the point where their reaction to their difficulties in to fabricate or induce illness in their child;*

- *Enquiries under section 47 of the Children Act 1989 may reveal significant unmet needs for support and services among children and families, particularly in relation to the needs of the parents and the way on which the family members relate to each other. These should always be explicitly addressed if the family members so wishes, even where concerns are not substantiated about significant harm to a child;*

---

10 HM Government 2006

11 Department of Health et al 2000

12 The guidance was issued under S.7 of the Local Authority Services Act 1970 requiring local authorities to act under the general guidance of the Secretary of State.

- *If safeguarding children processes are to result in improved outcomes for children, then effective plans for safeguarding and promoting each child's welfare should be based on a wide-ranging assessment of the needs of the child and their family circumstances, taking account of past histories of all family members.*

- *All work with children and families should retain a clear focused on the welfare of the child. Just as safeguarding children processes should always consider the wider needs of the child and the family, so broad-based family support services should always be alert to, and know how to respond quickly and decisively to potential indicators of illness being fabricated or induced in a child*[13].

The Guidance reiterates at many points throughout, the importance of information sharing and the following are set out as pointers to what professionals should be alert to if the guidance is followed properly;

- *Be alert to potential indicators of illness being fabricated or induced in a child;*

- *Be alert to the risk of harm which individual abusers, or potential abusers, may pose to children in whom illness is being fabricated or induced;*

---

13 Para 1.5 of the 2008 Guidance https://www.londonsafeguardingchildrenprocedures.co.uk/files/sg_ch_fab_ill.pdf

- *Share and help to analyse information so that an informed assessment can be made of the child's needs and circumstances.*

- *Contribute to whatever actions (including the cessation of unnecessary medical tests and treatments) and services are required to safeguard and promote the child's welfare and*

  - *Regularly review the outcomes for the child against specific planned outcomes*

  - *Work cooperatively with parents unless to do so would place the child at increased risk of harm;*

- *Assist in providing relevant evidence in any criminal or civil proceedings, should this course of action be deemed necessary.*[14]

The importance of understanding what the procedural context should look like before FII forms part of a threshold or schedule of findings, is as important as understanding what to do afterwards. Much time and expense is spent on cross examination of experts by an advocate who has limited or no knowledge of the Guidelines and context with the end result of little effect. This applies regardless of which party is represented and whether an advocate is pleading the case or representing a parent or child. It is vital to know what should have been done and what should have been looked for.

Both the RCPCH and 2008 guidance make clear the circumstances that apply when considering any referral to Children's Social Care.

---

[14] Para 1.19 of the 2008 Guidance https://www.londonsafeguardingchildrenprocedures.co.uk/files/sg_ch_fab_ill.pdf

The 2008 guidance states that:

> *'Children's social care should decide and record, within one working day what response is necessary. From the point of referral, all professionals involved with the child and children's social care should work together. Lead responsibility for action to safeguard and promote the child's welfare lies with [children's social care] 'Referrals...may lead to no further action or to an initial assessment of the needs and circumstances of the child, and the provision of services or other help. If children's social care decides to take no further action at this stage, feedback should be provided to the referrer.'*[15]

The 2008 guidance goes on to give specific advice as to the action that children's services should take if there is cause to suspect the child is suffering, or is likely to suffer significant harm, setting out the process for the convening of a strategy meeting chaired by social services. Such meeting should include all of the key professionals who have been involved with the family in terms of the welfare of the child/ren.

Most importantly, from the point of view of the advocate;

> *'Children's social care also has lead responsibility for any core assessment and will co-ordinate the process of systematic information gathering to build up a medical, psychiatric and social history and an understanding of the child's needs and the parents' capacities to meet the child's developmental* needs.

---

15 Para 3.69 of the 2008 Guidance https://www.londonsafeguardingchildrenprocedures.co.uk/files/sg_ch_fab_ill.pdf

Children's social care should ensure that a comprehensive chronology of the child's history is compiled. 'Children's social care should work collaboratively with all other agencies currently involved with the child and family. In addition, it is likely to be necessary to contact agencies with past involvement in order to prepare a full history of the child's health and family situation.'

These passages from the 2008 guidance are necessary reading, providing a clear pathway for social workers once a referral has been made from health professionals. There is often much time before any proceedings are issued and a forensic analysis can be had but anyone instructed early on must be aware of these parts of the guidance and ensure, especially on the part of the parents or child, that the relevant disclosure is sought early.

A Local Authority advocate considering how to plead a case where there is suspected FII must also be alive to the duties identified by the guidance, not just in relation to medical professionals but also social workers and ensure that the pleadings/findings sought match the evidence and are not just repetition of suspicions that have not been closely enough analysed.

Too often it is the case that an advocate is asked to draft a schedule of findings which is then based on the social workers own assessment of matters that have been reported to them by health professionals which themselves have not been properly looked at and certainly not in line with either of the Guidance's. A considered schedule of findings will have forensically analysed the medical evidence, including the observations and communications alongside the medical aspects of treatment care and reporting. Although there is always the instruction of an expert to assist, the schedule usually is required much before the report has been received. There simply is no substitute to having an encyclopedic knowledge of the papers sooner rather than later. More consideration of how to do this is given in chapter 3.

Summary

It is easy for an unexperienced advocate to assume that the professionals have full knowledge of the processes and guidance that relates to them but in situations where cases such as these are few and far between, it is often difficult for professionals to identify and therefore apply or even have the basic training to identify that there may be FII or there may be something that looks like FII but lacks the intention required. Either way, the approach of the professionals can be critical to how a family is treated and how the family then respond back. Being suspected of fabricating your child's illness can make people respond in ways that appear damaging and lend weight to the appearance of alerting signs or the fact that there are significant other issues in the families' background that may be contributing to the presentations and reports are missed because there is a complete lack of understanding of the complexities and wider nuances around cases involving possible factitious illnesses or perplexing presentation. It is even more difficult for an advocate to even try to present a case or pick apart a case if they have limited knowledge of the same complexities and their interactions.

CHAPTER THREE

THRESHOLD AND FACT-FINDING

Cases involving alleged FII are notoriously difficult. The proceedings may have been issued because of concerns that cannot be pinpointed but are worrying enough to be thought to cross threshold. There are often a number of other concerns surrounding the family that justify the start of proceedings or there may well be the very real and highlighted concern of FII.

It is often counterintuitive for professionals to consider that parents or care givers, who in all other circumstances may seem to be appropriate and caring and loving, to be carrying out acts that are deliberately harmful to their child and it is also the case that in the most serious cases, the acts are carried out covertly, often while in hospital or other medical setting, making it even more difficult to identify.

Recognition of which type of FII is involved

There are two broad categories of cases involving FII, those whereby serious and sometimes life-threatening acts have been carried out on the child – the induced part. Then there are those where there has been a long and comprehensive history of what appears to be exaggeration, attention seeking behaviours, repeated medical appointments and requests for examinations and over medicalisation of the child/ren of the family.

The first are easy to identify because it is highly likely that the proceedings have been issued as a result of concerns that have been raised in the medical setting with little or no concerns beforehand. These are akin to the non-accidental injury type of care cases whereby the court and parties are clear that the factual matrix must be established before the proceedings can go any further, if at all. In these types of cases, the LA will already have a wealth of evidence from treating medical professionals who would have raised the alarm to begin with and the need for scrutiny of those reports is vital, rather than an assumption that they must be right. The gathering of the primary evidence at the beginning stage is imperative and must not wait for the representatives of parents to be asking for disclosure – the Local Authority should be making those enquiries as soon as the case comes their way and the advocate at the first hearing will do well to ensure that they understand what may be available and what will need disclosure orders.

In the case of **Re IB and EB [2014] EWHC 369 (Fam)**, Mr Justice Baker (as he was then) gave judgment in a case involving substantial delay from the police and the NHS Hospital Trust and acknowledged that the orders within that case for disclosure had been very widely drawn up, whereas focused disclosure orders would have achieved a much more timely response. It is difficult to know what to ask for if the details of the circumstances are not understood or known in detail by those drafting the orders. The key to any of these cases is the detail and the knowledge of the detail.

The details of the above case are also helpful in understanding the recognition of the other type of FII case that you are likely to come across. In that case, Baker J was dealing with a very young baby, E, who had suffered very unusual injuries, some of which had occurred whilst she was still in hospital. Her older sister had previously suffered from a fractured finger which had been explained by the parents and appeared at the time to be accepted by professionals that it was due to an unwitnessed accident. However, these proceedings were brought because the LA were seeking findings that one of the parents had caused the injuries to E and therefore the circumstances of the finger injury to her sister were also called into concern. The detail of the allegations against the parents were that one of the parents had caused the injuries to E with a view to inducing symptoms of illness or injury and that the other parent had failed to protect. The Local Authority in their schedule of findings rely on six injuries for which they had clear medical evidence of their existence, including evidence of a foreign body (cotton wool) found in E's oesophagus which the LA alleged had been pushed there by one of the parents due to non-accidental intervention. The LA relied on the number of unexplained injuries as a pattern of induced illness/injuries that had been caused by one person and that that person posed a significant risk to children.

After a lengthy fact-finding hearing, where the court heard from a number of witnesses and experts as well as the parents, the court gave the final crucial judgment;

> *"INDUCED ILLNESS*
>
> *186. At the outset, it was the local authority's case that the pattern of injuries sustained by the children indicated that this was a case of induced illness or injury. In closing submissions, Miss Cook and Miss Phillips identified a number of features from the history in support of this contention. I have considered all of these points. They rely in particular on the observation made by Professor Fleming that "the combination of observations which were not all available at the same time, and putting them together one raises the possibility of the fabricated or induced illness". They also cite the evidence of Professor Roberts, who was the first clinician to raise the possibility of induced illness. They point to the mother's unsettled history, including incidents of self harm, and her anxiety. They also cite some odd incidents in the history such as the fact that the parents had lost the record of the oxygen download carried out 27th December, and the video-*

recording of E's breathing difficulties on 2nd January.

187. Crucially, however, the local authority's case on this issue turned on the interpretation of a pattern of behaviour. Given my findings on the individual allegations of abuse, which though serious are substantially fewer than sought by the local authority, I do not think that the allegation of induced illness is proved on a balance of probabilities. It is possible that the mother may have inflicted the pharyngeal tear in order to mimic the symptoms of illness, but equally there may be other interpretations. I apprehend that there will be further assessments in which the issue of the mother's motivation for this behaviour will be fully analysed. In the circumstances, it is neither necessary nor desirable at this stage for the court to make a finding as to why this injury was inflicted."[16]

Preparation of the papers

Perusal of any judgment involving issues of FII will establish one clear and common thread – the level of detail that is gone into by the court and parties into the history of events or medical histories. Indeed, the level of detail surpasses that of any other area of family law and is both necessary and fundamental.

Baker J in Re IB identified some of the issues and challenges;

'79. I have mentioned elsewhere the crucial importance of experienced legal representation in these difficult public family law cases. This case presented special challenges, in particular (1) the highly unusual nature of E's symptoms, injuries and medical history; (2) the voluminous history, and (3) the deplorable

16 Re IB and AB paras 186 and 187

failure of the police and UHS to disclose substantial numbers of documents until after the start of the proceedings. It would have been impossible for this court to have coped without the assistance of all the solicitors and counsel for the parties, including those instructed to represent the Trust. I hope I may be forgiven for singling out counsel for the local authority. Miss Cook demonstrated the vital importance in these very difficult public law cases of the local authority being represented by leading counsel experienced in grappling with these types of problems, and of marshalling the case to be put before the court, and crucially in cross-examination, in particular of the experts and the parents. She was ably assisted by Miss Phillips who stoically but successfully took on the burden of keeping control of the ever-expanding documentation."[17]

It cannot be emphasised enough how important it is for the LA advocates to have the knowledge of the papers, the chronology, the identity of potential witnesses, the roles played by the professionals within the family and the dynamics. These cases require thorough and comprehensive preparation from start to finish. Having a forensic knowledge of the papers is a requisite and there is no substitute for going over and over the disclosure. There are so often clues that are missed if not looked at through the lens of the FII matrix, eg, repeated requests for intervention; an odd fascination with medical terms or information, odd timings, change of shift when focus is not quite on the child, multiple and continuous complaints that appear to have very little basis, multiple referrals to professionals all dealing with the same issue.

Daunting as it may seem to be representing the Local Authority in such cases, the same can be said of those representing parents. The same difficulties apply in relation to the forensic analysis of the

17 Re IB and EB [2014] EWHC 369 (Fam) para 79

voluminous medical material and witness statements from all the people involved with the family pre-proceedings. Parents under suspicion of FII will be scared or evasive, many of the events having taken place many years ago and the difficulties of trying to get parents to remember what was said at what appointment becomes a herculean task. The local authority schedule of findings is likely to be extremely long and detailed, making it difficult to explain and go through in detail. On the other hand, the parents' representatives have the benefit of having a wealth of information often that assists in piecing the jigsaw together that the Local Authority will not have as readily. It is as important to have early involvement with the parents as it is for the local advocate to be on board.

Pleading of thresholds and schedule of findings

Threshold documents and schedules of findings are almost always lengthy, detailed and complex. Responses by parents add to the complexity and length with an additional layer of information and context. A properly pleaded Re A[18] compliant threshold is a must and an advocate's ability to produce one is really tested in these cases. The need to ensure that the primary evidence is available and can be placed before the court, either in terms of an actual witness or through a contemporaneous document take on a much heightened dynamic when the detail in such cases is picked apart by all.

Physical harm, as always, is much easier to see and evidence. In addition it is important for practitioners to keep in mind the implications of a child taking on the belief that they are an ill person, by naturalising dysfunctional health views into their belief system and the impact of that on them long term. The findings sought then

18 Re A (A Child) [2015] EWFC 11

become much wider but all need to come back to the point that the harm alleged is caused as a result of the parent's behaviour/actions.

Relevant harm is considered in more detail in chapter 4 although its relevance to how a case is pleaded cannot be ignored and advocates must be alive to the RCPCH guidance on harm specifically, which are considered in further detail in the next chapter.

Pleading of failure to protect against a parent who is not the perpetrator has also become the normality. It is difficult to see how the LA can ignore such a possibility in all but the most obvious of cases where the other parent's participation in events has been non-existent. The courts determination of the credibility of the other parent and their attitude towards the often non-controvertible medical evidence is crucial in the courts assessment of this issue and those representing other parents need to be alive to this from the very beginning, understanding the need to take their clients through the evidence with a fine toothcomb, to advise and explain the implications and to continue this process as the evidence emerges.

Once again, continuation of representation is fundamental, not only in terms of the advocate having knowledge of the case, but the ability to respond to emerging evidence and form key relationships with clients whereby difficult and key advice is likely to be required.

Pleading of a threshold or schedule of findings with reference to FII is a difficult and often complex task. The advocate is being asked to comb through the evidence, often before the final reports of the experts have been obtained, and formulate a case as soon as possible. This is a complex task but also a very dangerous one if not done properly and with careful consideration. If the proceedings have been issued with the already known concern that there is some element of concern around FII, then the case is much easier to approach and prepare. However, sometimes those issues do not arise until after proceedings have been issued and the concern is identified or becomes clearer upon further disclosure.

Re X, Y and Z (Children) [2010] EWHC is an important, if uncomfortable read, and is a real lesson in understanding the need for knowledge and experience of the area. In this case the issue of FII or whether the mother had exaggerated and/or lied about the children's conditions which resulted in unnecessary appointments, admissions, examinations and tests did not become apparent until the Independent Social Worker raised the issue as part of her final assessment of the parents.

The initial threshold document did not include any reference to anything resembling FII and the concerns really centred around areas such as lack of engagement, low level neglect, poor school attendance and inappropriate sharing of information in front of the children, which were common themes throughout the chronological involvement of social services with the family. Despite the very lengthy history of involvement with medical professionals and despite a Child Protection Conference having taken place some five years before where child Z was placed on the Child Protection register under the category of risk, where there was a marked difference in the way that the parents perceived their child was markedly different to that of the medical professionals involved in his care and importantly, the recommendations made for there to be a named lead Consultant Paediatrician to oversee the continuity of Z's care and for all agencies to report any concerns or changes promptly to the Keyworker to ensure clarity and consistency.

The independent social worker identified a gap in the evidence surrounding issues of medical issues given the central issue for the family appeared to be centred around health.

However, the independent social worker went on to acknowledge that there were two possible interpretations of her concerns:

> *"On the one hand, the parents could be seen as conscientious, totally committed, well researched, persistent and determined to ensure their children receive the best possible care, that to which they have a right. On the other, and the way in which the social work statement could be interpreted, it might be inferred that they seek medical advice and intervention inappropriately, to excess and to the detriment of the children being overly anxious and even exaggerating or manufacturing medical conditions.'*[19]

The issue was compounded by the Guardian then agreeing with the concerns raised by the ISW and describing the issue as a *'rumbling issue of concern that has threaded through years of professional intervention that there has been a preoccupation of Mrs C with health issues, which may have impacted on her children'*[20].

As a result the LA sought an assessment from an independent medical expert to consider the children's medical records. That report was received and there is much said within the judgment from paragraphs 54 to 58 whereby the Judge comments on the very brief conclusions reached by the expert with very little reasoning to explain how he had reached those conclusions. Suffice to say, the expert concluded generally that it was not for him to report on whether the children had been presented too frequently for presentation (despite being instructed specifically to consider that specific issue), that the children often presented with minor symptoms that were not easily verifiable and which were taken at face value, that there were inconsistencies and unusual patterns of seeking medical attention for all three children in

19 Re X, Y, Z (Children) [2010] EWHC, para 33

20 Re X,Y,Z (Children) [2010] EWHC, para 35

respect of reported seizures which led to unnecessary and invasive investigations, including CT brain scans and that the mother had '*perpetuated concerns about many illnesses or allergies suffered by her children for which there is little or no objective evidence*'[21]. In essence the expert came to the clear conclusions that the children were being subjected to harm due to the false nature of the presentations to medical professionals by their mother and that there was a real risk of the children themselves becoming caught up in a trap of 'falsification' of illness going forward.

The fact-finding hearing was set up for 20 days with a witness template containing twenty-eight witnesses. The first few days of the hearing were taken up with discussions and the Local Authority then took the view that they would be seeking leave to withdraw their applications in respect of two of the children and provided a much reduced threshold in respect of Child Z. The main issue relating to Child Z centred around his eye condition and whether that had been falsified by the Mother and a different expert had reported and was due to give evidence in respect of that issue. After hearing the oral evidence of this expert, the Local Authority took the sensible view that it would no longer pursue those findings in relation to Child Z and sought to withdraw the application as well.

This case is unusual in some ways but is a prime example of the difficulties that can arise if a case with issues of FII is not considered properly and comprehensively on behalf of the Local Authority. It also show the immense hard work that goes into the representation of a parents and despite the burden of proof being on the Local Authority, this judgment shows the necessity for the parents representatives being just as prepared and knowledgeable as the other advocates. The court reminded itself a number of times that the LA had sought twice to remove the children form the care of the their parents and now were

---

21 Re X,Y,Z (Children)) [2010] EWHC, para 57

seeking compete withdrawal. Understandably there was much criticism of the approach taken by the Local Authority and in particular with reference to the date that the Local Authority convened a strategy discussion as per the 2008 Guidance and its relevance to the situation before the court at that fact finding hearing.

The court was highly critical of the local Authority for not following the 2008 Guidance even after the instruction of the expert and it appears that the parties were simply waiting for the report and its conclusions. The Judge was clear that had the strategy meeting been called after the initial concerns around FII were raised by the ISW and the Guardian, there would have been a collating of the children's medical histories and more importantly an opportunity for 'information sharing' which in this case became highly relevant as the parents produced three separate letters from the children's GP's confirming his view that there had not been any over medicalisation or exaggeration on behalf of the parents and that this was not a case involving any level of FII – a point the Local Authority accepted in their closing submissions. The importance on the processes outlined in the guidance for professionals becomes very apparent when considering how differently this case could have been from the time concerns were raised, even if unusually, during the proceedings, rather than before. Indeed, the Judge eventually ordered the Local Authority to pay a sum of £100,000 towards the publicly funded costs of the parents, a very unusual situation in any care proceedings.

On a separate note, the judgment was also highly critical of the other parties and their attitudes towards Dr M, whose report was agreed to be flawed in many aspects, yet no questions were ever put to him. The Judge was clear that it was incumbent on all parties to remedy the concerns, not just the Local Authority.

The importance of information gathering and analysis from an early stage is outlined in the 'lessons to be learned'[22] set out by the Judge in Re X,Y,Z. In essence the local authority must make sure that it carries out its own rigorous assessment of ensuring that the evidence being put before the court, when such serious allegations are made, that such evidence is capable of establishing that there has been fabricated or induced illness/injury. And secondly, reliance upon an independent expert is not enough. The Guidance provides for a process to ensure there is information sharing from all professionals involved with the child/ren and family and their views should also be used in the analysis of the evidence.

The matter of threshold was also considered in **Re SK (Perplexing Presentation/Fabricated or Induced Illness: PP/FII) [2022] EWFC 144** where HHJ Moradifar came to the very clear conclusions that after hearing all of the evidence and in particular from all of the health professionals involved with the children and family, he could ***not*** come to the conclusion that the Local Authority's allegations, which were over one hundred and eight paragraphs, amounted to falsification and exaggeration of the children's medical conditions or that there had been unnecessary medical and quasi medical investigations of the children. The Judge goes on further to consider whether or not the matters he is able to find – such as an exaggeration of the children's medical conditions to get blue badge even amounted to threshold. The Judge did make some really minor findings that did amount to the threshold being crossing but the more serious allegations were all found to have significant evidential difficulties in not being able to be linked to the children either suffering significant harm or if they were, that harm being attributable to the mother.

What is abundantly clear from the judgment is the Judge 's overall consideration of the wider canvas of the family's life, experiences and

22 Re X,Y,Z (Children)) [2010] EWHC, para 170.

the totality of the evidence. The Judge makes specific reference to this and refers to the evidence of Dr Rose, the jointly instructed Consultant Paediatrician who, in his oral evidence, warned against the dangers of 'bacon slicing' the evidence and was clear that all of the evidence needed to be considered. The Judge reiterated this approach and that of all of the authorities dealing with this point. The wider canvas is often referred to as being something the Judge has the advantage of, over and above any expert ever instructed in any care case. Whilst this is undoubtedly correct, it is also correct that the advocates also have access to the wider canvas, and the parents' representatives have an advantage in being able to ask direct questions of their clients along the way that may assist in the way that their cases are presented.

In Re X,Y,Z referred to in detail above, the Local Authority's change in stance came about after they had received the detailed statements of the parents which made some concessions but also provided much explanation as to many of the allegations which were pleaded against them and on further consideration of such explanations against the wider evidence available, the Local Authority took the clear view that the evidence that they were relying on in support of their findings was no longer capable of proving the allegations to the requisite burden and standard of proof.

Again it is notable in this judgment that one of the main health professionals working with the family was not invited to any of the Child Protection Conferences and if she had been, she would have shared her view that there were no concerns about the nature or frequency of the number of medical appointments for the child, that all attendances were appropriate and that she had made referrals that she thought necessary and based on information from many sources, not just from the mother.

Further legal considerations

In **Re BR (Proof of facts) [2015] EWFC 41,** Jackson J (as he was then) published a short judgment in a case involving a large number of fractures to a baby. The short judgment published does not deal with any of the facts of the specific case but does provide invaluable guidance in relation to three specific areas; proof of facts, evidence about a child's pain response and an analysis of generic risk and protective factors.

In considering the proof of facts, the court reminds family practitioners of the need for the court to make decisions based on evidence, not speculation or assumption. Worries and concerns are simply not enough and especially not at the stage of fact-finding. Much emphasis is made throughout this book on the need for scrutiny of the medical records as a whole. Often the perusal of observations by nurses or others can help to clarify or expand on a bigger picture then that which is being painted by results or responses to treatment. Evidence that may seem trivial can in fact turn a case to a very different conclusion and may well be missed if the bigger picture is ignored. That said, Jackson J was clear to reiterate that the burden of proof lies on the party bringing the allegations, it is not for the parents to show that the allegations are not true – it is for the LA to show that the allegations are capable of being proved. In this particular case, the submissions made on behalf of the Mother by her advocates were referenced by the Judge as an example of the care that is required when considering the evidence;

> *"Improbable events occur all the time. Probability itself is a weak prognosticator of occurrence in any given case. Unlikely, even highly unlikely things, do happen. Somebody wins the lottery most weeks; children are struck by lightning. The individual probability of any given person enjoying or suffering either fate is extremely low."*

I agree. It is exceptionally unusual for a baby to sustain so many fractures, but this baby did. The inherent improbability of a devoted parent inflicting such widespread, serious injuries is high, but then so is the inherent improbability of this being the first example of an as yet undiscovered medical condition. Clearly, in this and every case, the answer is not to be found in the inherent probabilities but in the evidence, and it is when analysing the evidence that the court takes account of the probabilities.

8. Each piece of evidence must be considered in the context of the whole. The medical evidence is important, and the court must assess it carefully, but it is not the only evidence. The evidence of the parents is of the utmost importance and the court must form a clear view of their reliability and credibility."[23]

The judgment also sets out a very helpful list of both risk and protective factors complied from material available from the NSPCC, the Common Assessment framework and the Patient UK Guidance for Health professionals as useful tool with which to provide a framework within which the evidence could be looked at.

<u>*Risk factors*</u>

- *Physical or mental disability in children that may increase caregiver burden*
- *Social isolation of families*
- *Parents' lack of understanding of children's needs and child development*

---

23 Re BR (Proof of fact) [2015] EWFC 41, para 7

- *Parents' history of domestic abuse*
- *History of physical or sexual abuse (as a child)*
- *Past physical or sexual abuse of a child*
- *Poverty and other socioeconomic disadvantage*
- *Family disorganization, dissolution, and violence, including intimate partner violence*
- *Lack of family cohesion*
- *Substance abuse in family*
- *Parental immaturity*
- *Single or non-biological parents*
- *Poor parent-child relationships and negative interactions*
- *Parental thoughts and emotions supporting maltreatment behaviours*
- *Parental stress and distress, including depression or other mental health conditions*
- *Community violence*

Protective factors

- *Supportive family environment*
- *Nurturing parenting skills*
- *Stable family relationships*

- *Household rules and monitoring of the child*
- *Adequate parental finances*
- *Adequate housing*
- *Access to health care and social services*
- *Caring adults who can serve as role models or mentors*
- *Community support*[24]

Expert assessment

Expert assessment, once within proceedings, is always going to be required given that the majority of parents will be contesting. A Consultant Paediatrician will always be the first expert to consider and there are very few that are experienced enough in FII cases. Some of these particular experts are confident and able to prepare medical chronologies to go along with their reports but nothing substitutes the preparation of a comprehensive medical chronology – this does not always have to be prepared by the advocates and there are many reputable companies who are able to prepare detailed medical chronologies. It really depends on the level on medical involvement for each case and how time consuming and complex the issues may be. The more health professionals involved, the more likely it is that the number of appointments, interventions, treatments etc there are, the longer a chronology will likely be.

Early preparation of a chronology will allow an advocate to consider the medical evidence in an organised way, which might establish any

24 Re BR (proof of facts) [2015] EWFC 41, para 18

patterns of behaviour or show evidence of other factors that are relevant and not easy to see in thousands of pages of medical records alone. In cases where there is already much disclosure, if the Local Authority have not already commissioned such a chronology before the first hearing, insist on one being done as son as possible.

Word of mouth goes a long way and asking around colleagues for recommendations and experiences cannot be underestimated. Perusal of the judgments concerning FII will also give clear guidance as to those experts who assisted the court as opposed to those who perhaps were not as helpful.

The identity of other experts will really depend on the specific medical issues at the heart of the individual case. Often there is a need for an adult psychological or psychiatric assessment of the alleged perpetrator. Other experts can be wide and varied and are really relevant when it comes to medical issues which are disputed between the already involved health professionals. Remember, treating medical and health professionals are not jointly instructed independent experts and where there is call for clarity, make the necessary Part 25 applications.

In the X,Y,Z case, the ophthalmologist's oral evidence resulted in the LA abandoning their case in respect of child Z. In **Lancashire County Council v TP [2019] EWFC 30** the instructed experts included a well-known and respected Consultant Paediatrician, an adult psychologist and a Consultant psychologist specialising in gender identity. The issues in this case were very different to the usual FII cases before the court included, but were not limited to, concerns about the relevant parents acting in a 'precipitate manner' regarding perceived gender dysphoria in children they were caring for. After receipt of the expert reports, the Local Authority reconsidered their position and sought to withdraw the proceedings, recognising that the original threshold document they had been relying on could not be pursued as originally formulated in light of the expert's conclusions and that it was agreed that the children should remain in the care of their family with no need for any orders.

In line with the approach to be taken when a Local Authority are seeking to withdraw at this stage of proceedings[25], the Local Authority argued that there were still limited aspects of the threshold that they submitted were capable of being proved and if proved, could show that the children had suffered significant harm as a result of the parenting received. In those circumstances the court is required to conduct a nine-point analysis before considering whether permission to withdraw should be granted. The breadth and scope of that nine point analysis is beyond the scope of this book and the salient points of this judgment really come down the level of detail taken by the experts in their assessments and their conclusions overall that there was no evidence of inappropriate use of health services, no evidence of fabrication or induction, and significantly no evidence of the relevant parents seeking specialist opinions, suggested developmental or mental health diagnoses or gender dysphoria referrals. Indeed, Dr Pasterski, the gender specialist psychologist went as far as to say that he found it impossible that there had been any potential influence of fabricated or induced illness in relation to gender dysphoria, ASD or ADHD by the parents as each had a basis in neurological/biological functioning and that they could not be affected by interpersonal or environmental influence or interference.

The case is unusual in terms of the areas that came to be considered and the Judge acknowledged this by commenting as follows:

> 1. *I do not consider it a proportionate or appropriate exercise within the confines of this hearing and this judgment to express*

---

25 A Local Authority v X, Y, Z (permission to withdraw) [2017] EWHC 3741 (Fam)

> *any concluded views on how it was that these proceedings commenced. I observed during the course of the hearing that issues relating to gender identity and the medical understanding of such issues is complex and developing and that inevitably there is some lag between those professionals at the cutting edge such as Dr Pasterski and others (in which I include myself), which might have played some role in how these proceedings came about. Beyond that, as I indicated to Ms Cheetham QC at the IRH, I will not venture.*[26]

The difficulties with the instruction of an expert who is not experienced enough or qualified to carry out the specific and specialised assessment was highlighted in Re X and as part of the lessons to be learnt, HHJ Bellamy reiterated the following:

> *(c) When instructing an expert to prepare a report in a case of suspected FII the letter of instructions should make it clear that the expert is expected to have regard to 'Fabricated or induced illness by Carers (FII): A Practical Guide for Paediatricians' published by the Royal College of Paediatricians and Child Health in October 2009 and should also draw the expert's attention specifically to the guidance on 'Content of the Expert's Report' set out at paragraph 3.3 of the Practice Direction: Experts in Family proceedings Relating to Children.*

> *(d) As stated by Charles J in Re R (Care: Disclosure: Nature of Proceedings), all those involved should consider and review the report of an expert when it is received and, where relevant, raise points with the expert and other parties relating to the performance of the expert's instructions, his or her reasoning,*

---

26 Lancashire para 81

the factual basis of his or her views and the relevance of his or her views to the proceedings.[27]

Covert Recordings

A covert recording is one which has been made without any permission or knowledge of the person being recorded. It applies to both audio and visual recordings. In themselves they are not illegal if made in a private capacity (see below for surveillance by public bodies) but are not immediately admissible as is the usual course of action within public law proceedings. Inevitably in the circumstances that we are talking about, the recordings are likely to involve children, often without their permission.

Recordings by parents/carers

Often it is a parent who has carried out covert recordings and wants to rely on them. That situation has a very different legal context. Consideration of the relevant case law[28] (the majority of which relates to private law disputes) indicates that there has been a two-pronged approach to any application by a party to rely on covert recordings, whether video or audio;

A) The relevance of such recordings to the issues in the case;

27 Re X para 170

28 See Re: Children (Private Law: Covert Recordings: Adjournment if Final Hearing) [2021] 11 WLUK 543 and M v F (Covert Recording of Children) [2016] 4 WLR 92

B) Is the evidence which the application relies upon the whole of the evidence, ie, is it an accurate representation?

In December 2022, following an invitation from Sir James Munby in **Re B (A Child)**[29] the Family Justice Council formed a working group that considered this matter in detail. They published their guidance in December 2018[30]. The Guidance is not meant to be a routeway for covert recordings to form part of proceedings but instead emphasises the potential for harm to the child/ren.

The words of The Honourable Peter Jackson in M v F[31] must be borne in mind when considering the guidance, in that it is almost always likely to be wrong for a child to be recorded without their knowledge for the purposes of gathering evidence in family proceedings. The distinction between here is that it is highly likely that the covert/overt recordings have taken place before proceedings were even contemplated as a reality by the person taking the videos. Yet the identified difficulties in M v F remain a serious consideration;

A) The damage to adult relationships;

B) The implications of the recorder being unable to trust/work with professionals going forward;

C) Creating a secret between the adults and child/ren.

The main benefit within care proceedings is the fact that a child is already represented and has a guardian appointed.

---

29 Re B (A Child) [2017] EWCA Civ 1579

https://www.nagalro.com/_userfiles/pages/files/covert_recording_guidance_for_consultation_final_91122.pdf

31 M v F (Covert Recording of Children) [2016] 4 WLR 92, para

Covert Video Surveillance

In some very rare cases, whereby there is suspicion of fabrication/inducement there may be consideration by the professionals involved of whether there needs to be covert video surveillance of the interactions between the child and the carer to ascertain whether or not abuse is occurring. This circumstance is always likely to happen before any proceedings are instituted and must involve the triggering of a referral to social care first. The use of covert surveillance is not an easy process and is governed by the **Regulation of Investigatory Powers Act 2000.**

The Act regulates the ability of public bodies like Local Authorities in using covert surveillance. It is Part II of the Act that applies to these situations and an advocate will do well to be knowledgeable about what is permitted and the circumstances under which such surveillance can be obtained.

First and foremost is that the surveillance must have been considered by all professionals to be the only way of obtaining evidence as to the child's symptoms/condition which cannot be explained in any other way despite attempts to do so. The decision should only be taken after a Multi-Agency Strategy Discussion and there should be clear evidence of the routes taken beforehand and the reasons why the suspicions fall to exaggeration and/inducement.

Any application for authorisation of covert surveillance is the responsibility of the police and they are also responsible for the operations/s themselves, not relying on health professionals or social workers to do this. However, any criminal matters take second place and the clear purpose of the surveillance is to establish if harm is being caused and how. The Local Authority must always be prepared with a contingency plan for safety if the surveillance shows the child at risk of being harmed or being harmed.

Intimate Images

Special consideration will also need to be had in line with 'intimate images" – "*an image of a person, whether an adult or a child, naked or partially naked. Such an image can include part of a person's body, clothed or unclothed, such as breasts, genitalia or the anus, which are generally regarded as private. Intimate images include those of a person engaged in what is normally regarded as private behaviour such as washing, urinating, masturbating or engaged in other sexual acts either alone or with another being.*"[32]

Although Mrs Justice Knowles gave her general observations on the use of intimate images in the context of private law proceedings, the observations are relevant to cases involving FII whereby carers take photos of their children to try to prove to medical professionals or others that what they are reporting is true. These may be completely valid or they may constitute abuse. Rarely will they be done with the consent of the child.

The observations are lengthy but require consideration in any case whereby intimate images are going to be used, with the emphasis on intimate not just being based around sexual images or the genital parts of the child's body.

> *a) Sexually explicit or intimate videos and photographs should not be filed as part of evidence without a written application being made to the court in advance.*
>
> *b) Any such application will require the court's adjudication, preferably at an already listed case management hearing.*

[32] Re M (Private Law Children Proceedings: Case Management: Intimate Images) [2022] 1 WLR 4297, para 47.

c) It is for the party making such an application to persuade the court of the relevance and necessity of such material to the specific factual issues which the court is required to determine.

d) The court should carefully consider the relevance of the evidence to the issues in the case together with the likely probative value of any such evidence.

e) As part of its analysis and balancing exercise, the court will need to consider all the relevant factors including (i) any issues as to vulnerability in relation to any of the parties and the likely impact on any such parties of the admission of such evidence and the manner in which it is used in the proceedings; and (ii) if it is able to do so at a preliminary stage, whether the application/use of such images is motivated, in whole or in part, by a desire to distress or harm a party.

f) The circumstances in which a court will permit the inclusion in evidence of sexually explicit or intimate videos or photographs of any person are likely to be **rare**, *in particular, in circumstances in which that person does not consent to such material being admitted.*

g) Where the court is being asked to admit such material, the court should consider whether there may be a range of alternatives to the viewing of such material, for example but not limited to:

i) seeking an admission/partial admission in respect of the alleged conduct

ii) agreed transcripts and/or descriptions of any videos

iii) playing only the audio track of any video recordings

iv) using a still image rather than a video or a short excerpt from a longer video

v) editing images to obscure intimate parts of the body

vi) extracting meta data as to the timing and location of the evidence

vii) focused and specific cross examination on the issues

viii) consideration of the use of other evidence to prove the particular fact in issue instead.

h) If the court decides to admit any sexually explicit or intimate images/videos for any purpose, care should be taken to limit the volume of such evidence to that which is necessary to fulfil the purpose for which it is admitted;

i) The court should determine who can view the material that is to be admitted and limit this where necessary, bearing in mind its private character and the humiliation and harm caused to those both depicted and involved in the proceedings;

j) If the evidence is considered relevant, a starting point should be to say that it should incorporate the lowest number of images, seen by as few people as necessary, and viewed in the least damaging way;

k) It would be helpful to consider how best to ensure that the evidential security of such material can be maintained (for example, by using only password protected files) both within the hearing itself and outside it, and how the material is deployed within the proceedings;

l) Likewise, specific consideration should be given to the protection and safeguards necessary in respect of any video evidence relied upon (for example, such evidence being made available on a single laptop and brought to court, or the distribution being limited to a core specified legal team on behalf of each party). [33]

Summary

These are often the most complex cases before the court. They are incredibly hard to prove and require careful management from the very beginning. Anything less is likely to result in the manifestation of significant problems later. Careful management is required, not just of the evidence which is often voluminous, repetitive and difficult to interpret by non-medical professionals but of the way in which the case is pleaded.

Pleading threshold/findings sought is an arduous job and requires as much thought as the evidence that is available and the bigger picture. Even if there is evidence of fabrication in relation to other issues, that does not automatically translate to 'fabrication' for all medical issues and advocates and other professionals should steer clear of the assumption approach. A careful consideration of each issue is required with an open mind on each. Often these families have multiple medical/health issues and it is not necessarily the case that each is fabricated or exaggerated. Often the pleadings will not explicitly indicate that this is an FII case given the clear move away from labelling;

[33] Re M (Private Law Children Proceedings: Case Management: Intimate Images) [2022] 1 WLR 4297, para 77.

175. The terms 'Munchausen Syndrome by Proxy' and 'Factitious (and Induced) Illness (by Proxy)' are child protection labels that are merely descriptions of a range of behaviours, not a paediatric, psychiatric or psychological disease that is identifiable. The terms do not relate to an organised or universally recognised body of knowledge or experience that has identified a medical disease (i.e. an illness or condition) and there are no internationally accepted medical criteria for the use of either label.

176. In reality, the use of the label is intended to connote that in the individual case there are materials susceptible of analysis by paediatricians and of findings of fact by a court concerning fabrication, exaggeration, minimisation or omission in the reporting of symptoms and evidence of harm by act, omission or suggestion (induction). Where such facts exist the context and assessments can provide an insight into the degree of risk that a child may face and the court is likely to be assisted as to that aspect by psychiatric and/or psychological expert evidence.

177. All of the above ought to be self evident and has in any event been the established teaching of leading paediatricians, psychiatrists and psychologists for some while. That is not to minimise the nature and extent of professional debate about this issue which remains significant, nor to minimise the extreme nature of the risk that is identified in a small number of cases.

178. In these circumstances, evidence as to the existence of MSBP or FII in any individual case is as likely to be evidence of mere propensity which would be inadmissible at the fact finding stage (see Re CB and JB supra). For my part, I would consign the label MSBP to the history books and however useful FII may apparently be to the child protection practitioner I would caution against its use other than as a factual description of a series of

> *incidents or behaviours that should then be accurately set out (and even then only in the hands of the paediatrician or psychiatrist/psychologist). I cannot emphasise too strongly that my conclusion cannot be used as a reason to re-open the many cases where facts have been found against a carer and the label MSBP or FII has been attached to that carer's behaviour. What I seek to caution against is the use of the label as a substitute for factual analysis and risk assessment.*[34]

There is then the management of any fact-finding hearing which is highly likely to involve many many witnesses aside from any instructed experts and the parents. Witnesses from medical settings that may have moved to a different employment, may not be available any longer or may not want to be involved or cooperate. Although it is the Local Authority who are bringing the case and the allegations in particular, it is the reliance on outside witnesses that becomes more difficult. The very nature of these families means that there is often a deluge of professionals involved, each with slightly different roles but each contributing to the factual matrix and the wider canvass that the advocates and ultimately the court must navigate and unpick in determining the truth of the matter. The key is remembering that the Judge, who was not present at the time of the incidents alleged, cannot therefore '*determine what did happen as a matter of objective truth*'[35] and instead must look at the totality of the evidence, including the wider canvass. Mrs Justice Knowles went on in the case of Re Y to make some observations about case management in cases involving FII. These observations can be summarised as follows:

---

34 Re X,Y,Z paras 175 – 178.

35 Re Y (A Fact Finding: Fabricated Induced Illness) [2018] EWHC 4020 (Fam), para 5.

- It is important for those instructed to grapple with what is required on an evidential basis early on;

- The complexity of these cases require ALL advocates to give careful analysis and keep this going at each and every stage;

- The early collection and disclosure of medical and health records and statements from relevant personnel involved is vital;

- Early identification of expert evidence should also be done as soon as the issues in the case are clear and in these types of cases, the issues requiring expert and what type of experts tends to be obvious because of the nature of medical issues;

- Given that it is highly likely that a Consultant Paediatrician is almost always instructed, the letter of instruction MUST seek clarification from the expert for early identification of any other experts that may be advised.[36]

It is easier in many ways to deal with those cases whereby the allegations are of inducement or actual harm whilst in hospital or in a medical setting but the covert nature of many of the acts and behaviours still require a forensic approach and it must be kept in mind that proving a covert act is not an easy task for any advocate. Often it is a diagnosis of exclusion as can be seen in the discussion of the many cases above where the local authorities resorted to having to accept they could not prove their case and sought to withdraw the applications.

---

36 Re Y, paras 11 – 15.

CHAPTER FOUR

POST-FACT FINDING

The majority of judgments dealing with FII cases are those relating to the fact-findings stage of proceedings. It is difficult to see many situations whereby the court can carry out a combined fact-finding and welfare hearing although it is not impossible and can be done in certain cases. Determination of the factual disputes are usually the first and foremost priority as these are often single-issue cases and many will drop away if the factual findings or threshold are not met or made out.

Once the factual matrix has been stablished and if findings are made, the court will allow time for the parents to consider the judgment in full and for the parties to consider the way forward in terms of case management and whether further assessment is required. This is a crucial period for the representatives of parents against whom serious and significant findings have been made. It requires much skill and patience to counsel a client in such circumstances in order to lead them to a position whereby a future can be seen. Acceptance is going to be fundamental to any assessment going forward and the right expert for the right client and situation is a must.

The approach is a very different animal at this stage of the proceedings and the experts therefore must reflect that. However, all of the points made in chapter 3 above in relation to experts applies equally.

The relevance of the findings within the family dynamics is a fundamental aspect of the progression and ultimate care plan/s. The impact on other children within the family is an additional factor and one that must not be overlooked, having had an intense focus on the factual matters for so long.

Harm to children

The RCPCH guidance sets out three areas of harm that should be kept under consideration. These are important because it is not the FII itself that is the harm but the effect of the FII that causes the harm. Explaining that to a distressed client can in itself be distressing and difficult.

The health of the child and his/her experience of medical professionals/settings and healthcare

Findings by the court may include that the child has undergone repeated (unnecessary) medical appointments, examinations, investigations, procedures and treatments. The court may have gone further to find that the child found these to be as physically and psychologically uncomfortable or distressing

There may have been a genuine illness may have been overlooked by doctors due to repeated presentations or ignored because the fear of exaggeration or inducement meant the issue was not pursued;

There may have been actual illness or symptoms induced by the parents (eg poisoning, suffocation, withholding food or mediation) with potential or actual life threatening consequences.

Effect on child's development and daily life

There may be findings that the found behaviours/actions had an effect on the child's development and daily life, for example, there may have been:

- Reduced or interrupted school attendance and education
- Limitation to daily life activities due to over medicalization
- social isolation

Child's psychological and heath related wellbeing

- The anxiety or confusion experienced by the child about how ill they actually are or what they even suffer from.
- There may well have been a developing of a false view of themselves as being sick and vulnerable. The Guidance refers to adolescents who are likely to become more encompassed in this view and become caught up in a circle of false beliefs fueled by internet searches, social media or peer groups.
- The child may find it difficult to depart from the previously entrenched view of their parent that they are ill and there may be 'active collusion'.

What now?

The relevance to threshold is clear but any threshold must be drafted with the future progression of a case in mind and an understanding of how findings, if made or not made, will assist any assessments going forward. That is not to say that findings should be pleaded on the basis of steering a case towards a certain direction, indeed the opposite is a fundamental part of a local authority pleading. The Local Authority are not prosecuting a case, they are putting the evidence as they see it before the court. It is the court that is the ultimate tribunal of fact.

The wider family dynamics which will undoubtedly form part of the fact-finding hearing will also play a role within the future assessments and it may be that there are damaged relationships and dynamics between siblings or siblings and the parents that will require assessment and careful thought going forward. above list in not exhaustive but provides a comprehensive basis for consideration of any threshold and practitioners must always be alive to the fact that there may be other forms of harm that are unique to the child/family. The RCPCH guidance also talks about the rare occurrence of spousal or animal abuse having occurred in the more severe cases.

The judgment given by HHJ Moradifor in **Re C (Children: Fact find medical presentation)**[37] has already been considered but it is worth considering this in this chapter alongside the judgment from the second part of those proceedings **Re C (No 2)** [38]. In the first judgment, the Judge made a number of findings;

---

[37] Re C (Children: Fact Find Medical presentation) (Rev 1) [2020] EWFC B1

[38] Re C (Children: Welfare)(No.2) [2020] EWFC B 36.

A. *The mother has failed to maintain and promote a positive relationship between the children and their father by;*

   i. *Portraying the father and his wife negatively and speaking disparagingly about them in front of or within the earshot of the children, and*

   ii. *Wrongly holding a rigid view that the children have been emotionally abused by the father and his wife. The mother has exposed the children to these views, and*

   iii. *Asserting that the cause of A's FND behaviour and B's 'separation anxiety' related to contact with father in circumstances where such behaviour was much reduced when A was in the care of his father, and*

   iv. *Seeking to explain B's 'separation anxiety' by reference to his contact with the father.*

B. *The mother removed A from school in December 2016 and B in November 2017 without any good reason for doing so and subsequently failed to ensure that the children received adequate, consistent and appropriate education.*

C. *The mother was unable to*

   i. *manage A's behaviour, to put in place appropriate boundaries and maintaining the same, and*

   ii. *protect B from A's behaviour that caused B significant anxiety, distress and concern for the mother's safety that in turn created further anxiety about attending school and leaving the mother alone with A, and iii. appropriately address B's anxieties.*

D. The mother has been anxious and rigid in her quest for certainty and detailed information about any perceived medical condition that the children may have had. This has led to;

i. Above average presentation of the children to treating medics, and

ii. Open discussions about medical conditions in front of the children, and

iii. Over anxious attention to the children's medical and health needs within and outside of the home, and

iv. Over anxious pursuit of medical diagnosis and employing strategies to deal with undiagnosed conditions such as ADHD, Dyslexia, Grapheme Colour Synaesthesia, and

v. Children's home circumstances being dominated by medical issues and the children living in an environment of deficit and negativity with little hope of recovery from the perceived medical conditions, and

vi. At times A assuming a 'sick role' to control his home environment and those individuals within the home, and

vii. The children's home environment and the mother's inability to cope with the same has led to an increase in A's psychogenic and FND behaviour who has since 2017 expressed suicidal ideation, and viii. At times B's needs not being met and forgotten, and

ix. During these periods of significant stress and anxiety, the mother's ability to make appropriate decisions for the children has been significantly compromised.

E. The mother is unable to reflect or demonstrate any meaningful insight into the impact of her behaviour as found in above paragraphs (save for paragraph C ii.) on the children.

F. The mother clearly loves her children and I do not find that any of her conduct as I have found and set out above was intended to harm her children.

It is important to consider the level of detail that the Judge went into in making his findings as although the Local Authority did not plead the case as one of FII specifically, they did allege, amongst others, that the mother had misrepresented, administered unrequired medications/treatments and held entrenched views that were different to the medical professionals involved.

The interplay of the wider canvas is easy to see in this case with the difficulties between the parents having contributed to some of the behaviours and anxieties by the mother. However, the Judge went further in considering the actions/behaviours of Child A and the impact on the mother and family. This was as important as the findings made against the mother against a background of a recent ASD diagnosis when the case came back before the court for consideration of further assessment. The children were assessed by Great Ormond Street and the mother was assessed by an adult psychologist Dr Allam who made detailed recommendations of how the mother could be worked with to understand the findings that had been made and the proposed care plans for the children. Child B, who had always remained in the mother's care, was thriving and it was agreed he would remain there. Child A was a much more complex situation and the findings made at the fact-finding were relevant to the assessment by GOSH and the ultimate care plan for him to remain at his current residential placement while further work was carried out with him. A proposed plan of comprehensive family therapy was identified by Dr MacDonald at GOSH which would cover the areas identified at the fact-finding and provide the basis for work to remedy the damage already done.

This a contrast to the case of **Re X (Factitious Disorder) [2021] EWFC 46** where the court did unusually hear a fact-finding and welfare hearing together. The difference in this case was there had been previous proceedings and previous findings made against the mother of a very serious nature relating to FII which were not appealed and therefore remained. The threshold findings sought at this final hearing were many but included an allegation that the mother suffered from a Factitious Disorder, had done so in the past and continued to do so despite some periods where she presented better. Interestingly the Mother had been told many years ago, erroneously, that she suffered from Addison's disease, a medical condition which is life long and requires continued medication. The Mother had presented at hospital many times over the years with symptoms such as unconsciousness, semi-consciousness, vomiting, nausea and headaches that were consistent with the disease, however it became clear during the course of these proceedings that the Mother did not have Addison's disease and her symptoms really related to a somatic symptom disorder as these symptoms had no organic cause. Coupled with the chaotic lifestyle of the mother that involved criminality, becoming involved in volatile and abusive relationships and real concerns about her ability to parent, the Judge was able to find threshold met on many levels and despite some obvious progress that had been made in recent months, the Judge was clear that it was not enduring despite the support and treatment that had been available to her and therefore she could not care for the children.

Summary

Reunification despite serious findings of FII against a parent is still possible. Much depends on the nature of the findings, the acceptance of the parents, options of protective factors such as partners and other family members. Consideration of the treatment and support plan going forward are vital. Although psychotherapy is the main treatment for a person suffering from a Factitious Disorder, there must also be consideration of the wider issues, possibly more historical issues that may have led to the disorder manifesting itself. The need for a clear plan agreed by both family members and all professionals involved is vital. It is highly likely that some of the medical issues will remain, either for the children and possibly for the adult and there needs to be recognition for all those involved for what to look for and what to do in circumstances where there is concern that the behaviors are returning. Regular sharing of information between the professionals and identified protective family members will ensure that there is little opportunity to miss vital signs. Although this is not possible in all cases, thinking outside of the box is very much required in thinking about how rehabilitation can be achieved and sustained.

Conclusion

Factitious illness/disorder is a fascinating area in itself. When it presents with possible abuse or harm towards a child, it enters the realms of

All of the reported cases are clear that where there have been findings of FII, there has been some history of childhood or early emotional, physical or sexual abuse, trauma, illness and adverse experience of such, a significant bereavement or some other experience that has had a traumatic impact on the individual. This is not an exhaustive list but what is clear is that there is some form of trauma or stress impacts in such a way as to cause someone to behave in ways that are often counterintuitive to anyone around them, especially when the abuse is towards a child. The thought of someone deliberately harming a child to make them sick for attention is something most people, including health professionals will not want to believe and it is often sometime later, once the child has been exposed to physical and emotional harm alongside a whole battery of tests and treatments and examinations that suspicions start to arise.

Although meant to be pre-proceedings, the 2008 guidance sets out the approach which is also relevant to the second part of proceedings;

> *"There is no systematic research information available on the long-term outcomes for those carers who have received therapeutic help following identification of them fabricating or inducing illness in children (Bluglass, 2001; Brooke and Adshead, 2001). Some information is available from individual case studies (Nicol and Eccles, 1985; Black and Hollis, 1996; Coombe, 1995) and indirectly from research on outcomes for children. This means that decisions about the child 's safety have to be made on a case by case basis drawing on professionals' knowledge base about the abuse or neglect of children."* [39]

The need for compassion and understanding is as important when looking at the fact-finding part of the proceedings as it is once findings have been made. The 2008 Guidance has this at its heart and has a

---

[39] Para 2.34 of the 2008 Guidance https://www.londonsafeguardingchildrenprocedures.co.uk/files/sg_ch_fab_ill.pdf

real emphasis on the assessment of the wider needs of the family and a recognition that of any stress factors or histories with identification of support and services to move things forward. The move away from labeling allows the court and parties to consider the range of behaviours and to consider how best to deal with them going forward, allowing the focus to be on the child with safeguarding and welfare at the forefront of everyone's mind and moving away from the punitive stigma that was so often attached to 'Munchausen's' and 'Munchausen's by Proxy'.

'A Practical Guide to Hoarding and Mental Health for Housing Lawyers' by Rachel Coyle
'A Practical Guide to Psychiatric Claims in Personal Injury – 2nd Edition' by Liam Ryan
'Stephens on Contractual Indemnities' by Richard Stephens
'A Practical Guide to the EU Succession Regulation' by Richard Frimston
'A Practical Guide to Solicitor and Client Costs – 2nd Edition' by Robin Dunne
'Constructive Dismissal – Practice Pointers and Principles' by Benjimin Burgher
'A Practical Guide to Religion and Belief Discrimination Claims in the Workplace' by Kashif Ali
'A Practical Guide to the Law of Medical Treatment Decisions' by Ben Troke
'Fundamental Dishonesty and QOCS in Personal Injury Proceedings: Law and Practice' by Jake Rowley
'A Practical Guide to the Law in Relation to School Exclusions' by Charlotte Hadfield & Alice de Coverley
'A Practical Guide to Divorce for the Silver Separators' by Karin Walker
'The Right to be Forgotten – The Law and Practical Issues' by Melissa Stock
'A Practical Guide to Planning Law and Rights of Way in National Parks, the Broads and AONBs' by James Maurici QC, James Neill et al
'A Practical Guide to Election Law' by Tom Tabori
'A Practical Guide to the Law in Relation to Surrogacy' by Andrew Powell
'A Practical Guide to Claims Arising from Fatal Accidents – 2nd Edition' by James Patience
'A Practical Guide to the Ownership of Employee Inventions – From Entitlement to Compensation' by James Tumbridge & Ashley Roughton
'A Practical Guide to Asbestos Claims' by Jonathan Owen & Gareth McAloon
'A Practical Guide to Stamp Duty Land Tax in England and Northern Ireland' by Suzanne O'Hara
'A Practical Guide to the Law of Farming Partnerships' by Philip Whitcomb
'Covid-19, Homeworking and the Law – The Essential Guide to Employment and GDPR Issues' by Forbes Solicitors
'Covid-19 and Criminal Law – The Essential Guide' by Ramya Nagesh
'Covid-19 and Family Law in England and Wales – The Essential Guide' by Safda Mahmood

'A Practical Guide to the Law of Unlawful Eviction and Harassment – 2nd Edition' by Stephanie Lovegrove
'Covid-19, Brexit and the Law of Commercial Leases – The Essential Guide' by Mark Shelton
'A Practical Guide to Costs in Personal Injury Claims – 2nd Edition' by Matthew Hoe
'A Practical Guide to the General Data Protection Regulation (GDPR) – 2nd Edition' by Keith Markham
'Ellis on Credit Hire – Sixth Edition' by Aidan Ellis & Tim Kevan
'A Practical Guide to Working with Litigants in Person and McKenzie Friends in Family Cases' by Stuart Barlow
'Protecting Unregistered Brands: A Practical Guide to the Law of Passing Off' by Lorna Brazell
'A Practical Guide to Secondary Liability and Joint Enterprise Post-Jogee' by Joanne Cecil & James Mehigan
'A Practical Guide to the Pre-Action RTA Claims Protocol for Personal Injury Lawyers' by Antonia Ford
'A Practical Guide to Neighbour Disputes and the Law' by Alexander Walsh
'A Practical Guide to Forfeiture of Leases' by Mark Shelton
'A Practical Guide to Coercive Control for Legal Practitioners and Victims' by Rachel Horman
'A Practical Guide to Rights Over Airspace and Subsoil' by Daniel Gatty
'Tackling Disclosure in the Criminal Courts – A Practitioner's Guide' by Narita Bahra QC & Don Ramble
'A Practical Guide to the Law of Driverless Cars – Second Edition' by Alex Glassbrook, Emma Northey & Scarlett Milligan
'A Practical Guide to TOLATA Claims' by Greg Williams
'A Practical Guide to Elderly Law – 2nd Edition' by Justin Patten
'A Practical Guide to Responding to Housing Disrepair and Unfitness Claims' by Iain Wightwick
'A Practical Guide to the Construction and Rectification of Wills and Trust Instruments' by Edward Hewitt
'A Practical Guide to the Law of Bullying and Harassment in the Workplace' by Philip Hyland
'How to Be a Freelance Solicitor: A Practical Guide to the SRA-Regulated Freelance Solicitor Model' by Paul Bennett

'A Practical Guide to Prison Injury Claims' by Malcolm Johnson
'A Practical Guide to the Small Claims Track - 2nd Edition' by Dominic Bright
'A Practical Guide to Advising Clients at the Police Station' by Colin Stephen McKeown-Beaumont
'A Practical Guide to Antisocial Behaviour Injunctions' by Iain Wightwick
'Practical Mediation: A Guide for Mediators, Advocates, Advisers, Lawyers, and Students in Civil, Commercial, Business, Property, Workplace, and Employment Cases' by Jonathan Dingle with John Sephton
'The Mini-Pupillage Workbook' by David Boyle
'A Practical Guide to Crofting Law' by Brian Inkster
'A Practical Guide to Spousal Maintenance' by Liz Cowell
'A Practical Guide to the Law of Domain Names and Cybersquatting' by Andrew Clemson
'A Practical Guide to the Law of Gender Pay Gap Reporting' by Harini Iyengar
'A Practical Guide to the Rights of Grandparents in Children Proceedings' by Stuart Barlow
'NHS Whistleblowing and the Law' by Joseph England
'Employment Law and the Gig Economy' by Nigel Mackay & Annie Powell
'A Practical Guide to Noise Induced Hearing Loss (NIHL) Claims' by Andrew Mckie, Ian Skeate, Gareth McAloon
'An Introduction to Beauty Negligence Claims – A Practical Guide for the Personal Injury Practitioner' by Greg Almond
'Intercompany Agreements for Transfer Pricing Compliance' by Paul Sutton
'Zen and the Art of Mediation' by Martin Plowman
'A Practical Guide to the SRA Principles, Individual and Law Firm Codes of Conduct 2019 – What Every Law Firm Needs to Know' by Paul Bennett
'A Practical Guide to Adoption for Family Lawyers' by Graham Pegg
'A Practical Guide to Industrial Disease Claims' by Andrew Mckie & Ian Skeate
'A Practical Guide to Redundancy' by Philip Hyland
'A Practical Guide to Vicarious Liability' by Mariel Irvine
'A Practical Guide to Applications for Landlord's Consent and Variation of Leases' by Mark Shelton
'A Practical Guide to Relief from Sanctions Post-Mitchell and Denton' by Peter Causton

'A Practical Guide to Equity Release for Advisors' by Paul Sams
'A Practical Guide to Financial Services Claims' by Chris Hegarty
'The Law of Houses in Multiple Occupation: A Practical Guide to HMO Proceedings' by Julian Hunt
'Occupiers, Highways and Defective Premises Claims: A Practical Guide Post-Jackson – 2nd Edition' by Andrew Mckie
'A Practical Guide to Financial Ombudsman Service Claims' by Adam Temple & Robert Scrivenor
'A Practical Guide to Advising Schools on Employment Law' by Jonathan Holden
'A Practical Guide to Running Housing Disrepair and Cavity Wall Claims: 2nd Edition' by Andrew Mckie & Ian Skeate
'A Practical Guide to Holiday Sickness Claims – 2nd Edition' by Andrew Mckie & Ian Skeate
'Arguments and Tactics for Personal Injury and Clinical Negligence Claims' by Dorian Williams
'A Practical Guide to Drone Law' by Rufus Ballaster, Andrew Firman, Eleanor Clot
'A Practical Guide to Compliance for Personal Injury Firms Working With Claims Management Companies' by Paul Bennett
'RTA Allegations of Fraud in a Post-Jackson Era: The Handbook – 2nd Edition' by Andrew Mckie
'RTA Personal Injury Claims: A Practical Guide Post-Jackson' by Andrew Mckie
'On Experts: CPR35 for Lawyers and Experts' by David Boyle
'An Introduction to Personal Injury Law' by David Boyle

www.ingramcontent.com/pod-product-compliance
Ingram Content Group UK Ltd.
Pitfield, Milton Keynes, MK11 3LW, UK
UKHW020151290926
15471UKWH00004B/807

9 781914 608421